JEFF GORDON

PORTRAIT OF A CHAMPION

JEFF GORDON
PORTRAIT OF A CHAMPION

BY JEFF GORDON

WITH BOB ZELLER

HarperHorizon

An Imprint of HarperCollinsPublishers

Jeff Gordon: Portrait of a Champion was published by HarperHorizon,
an imprint of HarperCollins*Publishers* Inc. Horizon is a registered trademark
used under license from Forbes Inc.

HarperCollins books may be purchased for educational, business, or sales
promotional use. For information please write: Special Markets Department,
HarperCollins*Publishers* Inc., 10 East 53rd Street, New York, NY 10022.

FIRST EDITION

Designed by Gilda Hannah
Edited by Brian Silverman

ISBN 0-06-1073369 (paperback)
ISBN 0-06-1050849 (hardcover)

Printed in Canada

98 99 00 01 02 10 9 8 7 6 5 4 3 2 1

FOREWORD
BY BOB ZELLER

JEFF GORDON, in 1997, had one of the finest seasons in the history of the NASCAR Winston Cup Series. No driver has ever accomplished all that Jeff did in the 32 races that made up the 1997 campaign. He won everything that meant anything.

Behind the wheel of his rainbow-colored No. 24 Dupont Chevrolet Monte Carlo owned by Hendrick Motorsports, Jeff won his second Winston Cup championship. He won the Daytona 500. He won the Coca-Cola 600. He won the Southern 500 and became only the second driver to win NASCAR's toughest prize—the Winston Million. He won The Winston. He won the Busch Clash.

He won 10 races on 10 different tracks. He won at a superspeedway, a 2.5-mile speedway, a two-mile speedway, a 1.5-mile speedway, a one-mile banked track, a one-mile flat track, the "Lady in Black" at Darlington, both short tracks and a road course.

He did all of this in a season otherwise dominated by Ford drivers. And he did it in an era of unprecedented competition in stock car racing. When he won at Martinsville in April, the difference between winning the pole position and not making the race was about four-tenths of a second.

Other drivers have won more races in a year. They have established most impressive winning streaks. They have won their championships by wider margins. They have clinched the title earlier in the season.

But no one has ever achieved Jeff's record of all-around brilliance in 1997. Not only did he win on just about every type of track in the NASCAR Winston Cup Series, he won in just about every way a driver can win a race.

He won by passing the leader on the last turn of the last lap. He won by holding off a challenge from another driver on the last lap. He won a race by figuring out how to make the outside groove work. He won by sheer dominance in handling and horsepower. He won a gas mileage battle. He won under a yellow flag.

His domination of the season was so thorough and so frustrating to the fans of other drivers, particularly those of Dale Earnhardt, that Jeff began to elicit the same reaction golf fans had when Jack Nicklaus dethroned Arnold Palmer.

Nearly every week, Jeff was asked about the fans booing. And every week, he would face it straight up, sometimes with a chuckle or his boyish smile, and he would say that it was just part of the sport. "We just grin and wave and go on our way," he said.

Ironically, Jeff discovered, just as Earnhardt had a decade earlier, that the more fans booed, the more popular he became. His appearances were never more crowded than in 1997. He sold more collectibles than ever before. During the holiday season, his 1998 calendar maker had to go to press three times to satisfy the demand.

The impressiveness of Jeff's 1997 race record masks the excruciating struggle he faced to top it off with the NASCAR Winston Cup championship.

As it turned out, after he posted his 10th victory at New Hampshire International Speedway in early September, he did not win another race. Seven races remained after New Hampshire.

7

But in those final two months of racing, even though he did not win again, Gordon faced a challenge that would forever color not only the success of 1997, but the legacy of his first five years in the NASCAR Winston Cup Series.

Since entering the NASCAR Winston Cup Series in 1993, Jeff had been blessed with enough success to make two or three respectable careers for lesser mortals who race stock cars for a living.

He was the NASCAR Winston Cup Rookie of the Year in 1993. His first victory came in 1994 at one of NASCAR's major races—the Coca-Cola 600 at Charlotte Motor Speedway. Two months later, he won the inaugural Brickyard 400 at Indianapolis Motor Speedway.

In 1995, his third full season in the NASCAR Winston Cup Series, Jeff won seven races and his first Winston Cup championship. In 1996, he won 10 races.

But 1996 had ended with disappointment. He had owned the championship points lead most of the season, only to see it slip away to teammate Terry Labonte in the end.

Jeff had finished off the 1995 title with a whimper rather than a flourish, finishing 32nd at Atlanta, 14 laps behind the leader. He won the championship by 34 points over Dale Earnhardt. That did not please him.

And then the 1996 championship slipped away altogether. That setback gave Jeff and his team all the motivation they needed for the 1997 season. But it also put him at a distinct crossroad. He had won one championship. And he had lost one.

In 1997, after establishing himself as the dominant driver in the NASCAR Winston Cup Series for the third straight year, all Jeff had to do in the stretch run was finish it off.

If he failed, he would have been considered a driver who was known for winning races but failing to win championships. He would have established an impressive record of 27 race victories in three years and a not-so-impressive record of 1-2 in the championship.

There are great athletes and great teams in every sport who must shoulder this burden. In golf, it has been Greg Norman. In football, the Buffalo Bills play this role. In baseball, it has been the Atlanta Braves.

Had he lost the 1997 title, Jeff would have to win another two championships to fully erase the reputation of the superstar who couldn't get the job done when it really counted.

And that is why the season-ending NAPA 500 at Atlanta Motor Speedway on November 16, 1997, was the most important race of Jeff Gordon's racing life—the rubber match for five years' worth of racing stock cars. It was a genuine, 100 percent, American challenge.

The task seemed easy enough on paper, considering Jeff's 1997 record. All he had to do was finish 18th or better to win the title. The fact that he struggled to do it proved that Jeff and his team were human after all. But under the most intense pressure of his life, he did not let it get away. He won.

One could argue that it should not have come down to the Atlanta race; that Jeff should have already been celebrating his second championship before the final race.

As Mark Martin had said before the penultimate race at Phoenix: "If you look realistically at the things that Jeff and his team have done this year, they should be leading the points. They have outperformed us enough that they ought to be ahead of us."

But the NASCAR points system is like having a restrictor plate bolted on the championship. It is a great

equalizer. It forces the points leader to adopt a conservative strategy during the stretch run. It is not about winning, it is about surviving. Don't worry about winning the race. Just finish. No matter what.

It seems almost inhuman to make a racer race this way. A contender can sort of forget about the points for two-thirds of the season, but when summer turns to fall, and he's in contention, he has to temper all those normal racing instincts with the notion that winning is riskier than simply finishing well.

This is why The Winston often provides some of the wildest racing each year. The Winston is worth no points. It is a race where winning is everything. And it is no surprise that Jeff has won it two of the last three years.

It is also no surprise that a driver so successful at winning races would struggle to win a points champion-ship. Winning seems a natural thing to do for Jeff. Forced survival is another matter.

While the points system may not always be an accurate reflection of who deserves to be champion, it usually produces what NASCAR wants—a close battle to the bitter end.

As Jeff himself said at Phoenix, "It doesn't matter how many races you've won or how great a year you've had. That doesn't guarantee a championship. We won 10 races last year and didn't win the title. Anything can happen."

And in his case, at Atlanta, it did.

After a Friday rainout, Jeff took his car onto pit road on a cold Saturday morning and began sawing the wheel of his Chevy back and forth to put some heat in his tires, underestimating the hair-trigger temper of really cold tires.

Jeff spun his car and it slammed into Bobby Hamilton's Pontiac. Jeff's backup car should have been okay except the crew added a bit too much oil to the car before qualifying. A bit of it spilled onto Jeff's tires. He qualified 37th.

He raced a car named Backdraft, which seemed aptly named because he spent all afternoon driving in the backdraft of the leaders. But he did what he had to do. And he finished 17th. NASCAR got the tight points race it wanted, and Jeff got the championship he richly deserved.

The first championship will always have a special place in Jeff's heart and soul, but the second one was more important. He needed it to affirm all of his other stellar ac-complishments in 1997. He needed it to be able to call the first five years of his NASCAR Winston Cup career an unqualified success. And he had to wage the fight of his racing life to get it.

INTRODUCTION
BY JEFF GORDON

The year 1997 was certainly a year to remember for me and Brooke and Ray Evernham and all of the Rainbow Warriors. We won our second NASCAR Winston Cup championship and the Daytona 500 as well as nine other races and the Winston Million.

It wasn't like my first NASCAR Winston Cup championship in 1995, when we had the dominant car. We had the new Monte Carlo back then, and it seemed like we couldn't do anything wrong because the car was so unbelievably good.

Last year was different. Last year, we fought the Fords and we fought the Pontiacs a few times. Many times our DuPont Refinishes Chevrolet was the only Chevy battling those guys. It seemed like we were winning races when we probably shouldn't have been, when the odds were against us. If you look at the statistics, you see that Fords won most of the races. We felt like the Chevys were at a little bit of a disadvantage. So it's even more gratifying to have a year like we had.

To win the Daytona 500 was just an unbelievable way to start the season. The 500 turns into a race where the handling on your car is critical. And our handling was great. We had a great, great race car. But things got turned around pretty quickly when I cut a right rear tire. We almost lost a lap. I thought this was going to be another Daytona 500 where I just rode around and finished the thing. But we stayed on the lead lap. And then we won the race. That set the tone for the whole season. Winning the 500 taught us all over again, "Don't ever quit. Don't ever stop fighting. It's not over 'til it's over." That attitude carried us into the next race at Rockingham, which we also won. And it carried us all through the year.

The victory at Bristol was one of my all-time finishes. When I passed Rusty Wallace in the third and fourth turns of the last lap and won that race, it was like, "How did this happen?" That was probably the most excited I've ever been after a finish because my adrenaline was flowing and it came right down to that final corner. I was really expecting to run second because I just couldn't make the move to get up beside him. But when they threw that white flag, I saw some lapped cars ahead of us and I thought, "Man, if they hold him up, I might have a chance." Then we came off turn two and he bobbled a little bit and I was right on him. When we got into turn three, I just touched him slightly and he moved up and gave me just enough room to slide in there and get past him. It all came down so quickly.

At Martinsville, we spun and won after getting messed up with Jimmy Spencer. It wasn't like Danny Sullivan's spin and win at the Indianapolis 500, but it was pretty cool. Then we won the 600 again at Charlotte and came back from a flat tire to win at Pocono.

We won the inaugural California 500 at California Speedway, and that was the first time I've ever won a race with fuel mileage—where we had to conserve fuel to win.

And then we won at the road course at Watkins Glen. Of all the goals I set for myself for 1997, winning the championship was first and winning the Daytona 500 was number two. But the next one, really, was to win on a road course. It almost happened at Sears Point when we finished second to Mark Martin. At Watkins Glen, we didn't qualify very well, but all of a sudden I found myself tearing through the field. Winning that race was more personal than anything else. I wanted to prove to myself that I could win on a road course.

Before going to Darlington Raceway to race for the Winston Million in the Southern 500, I was telling myself that there was no pressure. But the opportunity to win the Winston Million doesn't come around very often. And because you're the only one going for it, there was a lot of pressure. But our team does well under pressure. It seems like when it's a big event or there's a lot up for grabs, we step up to the plate. The victory at Darlington was even better because we really had to race for it. It came down to the last lap and we managed to hold off Jeff Burton. Of course, we were running for a million dollars and I wasn't going to let him get by me without a fight.

When we got to Atlanta for the final race of the year, we wanted to win the championship as much as anything we'd ever done. When you have a year like we had, if we hadn't finished it off by winning the championship, it would have been very disappointing. It was a year that was meant for a championship.

I wasn't feeling a lot of pressure until I wrecked on pit road during Saturday morning practice. I'm not much of a morning person anyway. I remember saying on the radio, "Boy, it's so slick, somebody is going to wreck out here." It wasn't 15 or 20 minutes later and that "somebody" was me. I wouldn't have felt as bad had I just crashed by myself. But I took out Bobby Hamilton as well and that's why I felt so bad. I think I let that get to me. I got caught up in worrying about what Bobby and Richard Petty and their team were thinking. They were pretty unhappy with me. As hard as I tried not to let that affect me, I just couldn't control it. I had a pit in my stomach. And then I started to realize what a hole I had put myself in for the race.

I hardly slept at all the night before the race. I don't normally have that problem. I normally sleep like a baby the night before a race. But I felt better the next day. I told myself, "You know, win or lose, we're not going to give this

thing away. We're just going to have to go out there and fight all day long."

And that's exactly what we had to do. Our backup car wasn't that great. It was about a 15th-place race car. We needed to finish 18th or better to win the championship. Everyone was wound pretty tight, especially in the closing laps. I was out there running in about 15th place, complaining that the car was going away. Ray and the guys were in the pits looking at tire wear. And they saw that I was wearing my tires down to the cords. It looked like we might have to come in and make an extra pit stop. And that was exactly what we didn't want to do. The whole year, for us, came down to the final laps at Atlanta.

Those last few miles were excruciating. We hadn't been able to make a set of tires last 50 laps.

And I had to take that last set of tires and make them go 60 laps. I spent the last 10 laps trying to feel the tires under me. And I could feel them going away. They were all the way down to the cords. I was trying to keep them from blowing out. I was trying to keep from spinning out. I was just racing my own race. I stopped worrying about guys passing me and losing laps. Those last 10 laps took forever. You want it to be over and it seemed like it was never going to end. It seemed like the laps were going by slower than they ever had before. And they were. I think I drove that last lap the slowest of any lap all day. I don't think my tires would have lasted five more laps.

We finished 17th and won the championship by 14 points over Dale Jarrett. It would have been pretty disappointing to lose the

championship. It would have meant that we're not closers. And I think we still have a little bit to prove in that regard because we struggled at Atlanta the two times we won the title.

But we did win the championship. That's the important thing. We didn't lose it. We won it. That put the icing on the cake for all of the other things we did in the 1997 season.

The week of the banquet in New York in December is really when the accomplishment sets in. Everybody is talking to you about it. You get to reminisce about the whole season, and you see footage from the races, and you receive that championship check and trophy—that's when it all sinks in. And for me, it all sank in at once last year. But I definitely enjoyed the second championship even more than the first. It was just a

Brooke, Jeff, and Tom Cruise

whirlwind after that first one in 1995. I had no idea what was going on or what it really meant. After losing the championship in 1996, it made us realize this just isn't going to happen every year. So winning it again in 1997 was really gratifying. I got to enjoy it a lot more. It felt like we had set out to do something and then managed to accomplish it.

1997 was also a very busy year off the track. We had more fan mail, more requests for appearances, and more obligations to our sponsors and to the sport. My Tuesdays are usually reserved as media days or appearance days. Wednesday I go to the shop and the office. And Thursdays are another appearance day. Usually on Thursday, we'll be on our way to the race track and I'll do an appearance somewhere around there.

It's a very, very rare time when we don't have racing on our minds. But Brooke and I do get some time to ourselves, and Monday is our day to recuperate, kind of unwind, relax at home, and get

things done around the house. We unpack, sort through the mail, get caught up with phone calls, and sometimes go out to eat lunch. We have a couple of favorite restaurants—just small places near where we live. During the summer, we'll get out on the boat on Lake Norman. The lake is not too crowded during the week.

Brooke and I figure that we don't live permanently anywhere, except maybe at the race track. We spend more hours in our motor home than we do at our real home. I relax in the motor home with video games. Very seldom do I have time at home to play. I play more during the season than the off-season because I have time to play in the motor home. I have a TV in the back and I've got it all wired up. I play a lot of Sony Playstation games. I don't normally do much racing, but I'll do all the other different sports—baseball, basketball, football, soccer, tennis.

At some tracks, like Rockingham, Charlotte, and Martinsville,

we drive home after the race just like the fans do. We have to get right in the middle of all the traffic and then work our way home. I usually drive, and I've learned how to be patient with the traffic after the race as well as traffic in the race. We get spotted all the time and we wave, but we're on a mission to get out of there, just like everyone else is.

After a race, I'm usually starving. Sometimes I'll eat something on the plane. And sometimes Brooke will call ahead for pizza and have them have it ready for us on our way home. I try not to eat fast food very often, but sometimes I want the most filling thing I can find. After a race, I like things that are really salty. I'll eat a whole jar of olives or pickles. I believe the carbon monoxide you breathe in a race car takes a lot of your taste sensation away. So a lot of times I'll want something that tastes really strong.

When we get home Sunday night, we usually watch *RPM 2Night*. But it depends on the kind of day we had. Sometimes, if it's been a really bad race, we'll go to a movie—a comedy or something—so I can get my mind off it. Brooke and I are big movie buffs. We really enjoy that side of the entertainment world. One of the coolest things we did last year— actually it was one of the coolest things we've done of all time—was to go to the parties after the Oscar presentations in Los Angeles. We went as guests of TriStar Pictures. We were at their party and we met Woody Harrelson and Steven Seagal. Then we went over to the Vanity Fair reception and everybody was at that one: Tom Cruise, Jim Carrey, Steve Martin, Goldie Hawn, Winona Ryder, Leonardo DiCaprio. They didn't know who the heck I was. That was the coolest thing—talking to people like Tom Cruise and Chris O'Donnell. That was huge for us—to be able to be fans. It gave us a different perspective—something we don't get to see everyday. It meant a lot to us to meet those people and for them to be nice to us. Our hearts were fluttering. That's kind of the way some of my fans feel about me. So it definitely puts things in perspective, and how that first impression is really important.

It seems like every year it gets tougher and tougher to win in the NASCAR Winston Cup Series. The competition gets tougher and it's more difficult to make things go your way. To win the championship, you have to have cars that work well and a team that sticks together. You have to have engines that are working good and not falling apart. You have to qualify well. You have to avoid the wrecks. You never know what the next year is going to have in store for you. So you go out and work hard and just take it one step at a time.

Cindy Crawford, Jeff, and Brooke (inset).

THE BUSCH CLASH
DAYTONA INTERNATIONAL SPEEDWAY

It took Jeff Gordon 16 minutes, 11 seconds to win the year's first race, the 19th annual Busch Clash at Daytona International Speedway. In the first 10-lap segment, he started 13th and finished 12th. After the traditional halfway break and pit stop, the 14-car field was inverted for the final 10 laps. Jeff restarted the race in third place, directly behind leader Bobby Labonte.

"I knew the restart for the last 10-lapper really was going to be critical," Jeff said. "I got a great start. I gave Bobby Labonte a good push and then I got by him." Gordon took the lead with nine laps to go and that was that.

THE DAYTONA 500
DAYTONA INTERNATIONAL SPEEDWAY

After Jeff qualified sixth, he and his team settled into a week of practice to prepare for the Daytona 500, his fifth run in NASCAR's most important race. Here *(above),* he helps his team push his car back to the garage after a morning practice.

From his starting position on the outside of the third row, Jeff moved to the front and took the lead for the first time on lap 57. He was in front until lap 90.

"To win a championship, it doesn't just take great race cars, or a driver, or crew chief, or a team, *it takes everyone coming together;* everyone working toward a common goal."

On lap 110, Jeff was running in third place when he suddenly drifted high in turn two, slowed, and fell out of the draft. "Something just happened," Jeff told his crew on the radio. "It got real loose. I think I have a flat right rear tire." He made an unscheduled pit stop under the green flag to have the tire changed. The tire problem left Jeff stuck at the tail end of the lead lap. But he held off Mark Martin at the front of the pack until a yellow flag on lap 122 allowed him to make up most of the lost distance.

By lap 175, Jeff was back in the lead pack and ready to challenge for the victory. The climactic shoot-out came with just six laps to go, when Jeff and his teammates, Terry Labonte and Ricky Craven, ganged up on leader Bill Elliott, and Jeff took the lead.

On lap 197 the yellow flag flew for a 12-car crash among backmarkers in the fourth turn. The race ended under caution as Jeff, Terry, and Ricky crossed the finish line side by side by side. It was Jeff's 20th career victory, and his biggest.

Moments before emerging from his car, Jeff spoke with car owner, Rick Hendrick, on a cellular telephone. "This one is for you!" he shouted. The dramatic one-two-three finish by the Hendrick Motorsports Chevrolets was a triumph for Hendrick, who was at home in Charlotte battling leukemia. "This is the best medicine that the good Lord can give me right now," Rick said. All three drivers went to Victory Lane to celebrate the unprecedented feat.

THE GOODWRENCH 400
NORTH CAROLINA SPEEDWAY

Right and below: As the new Daytona 500 champion, Jeff was mobbed by the media when he suited up at North Carolina Speedway. But at Rockingham, the serious business of the long NASCAR Winston Cup season was just beginning. Behind the wheel, Jeff put on his game face.

Opposite: Although Jeff led this pack into turn one, Dale Jarrett dominated the Goodwrench 400. Of the first 350 laps, Jarrett led 323. All the while, Gordon struggled to find a groove on the one-mile banked track that worked for his Monte Carlo.

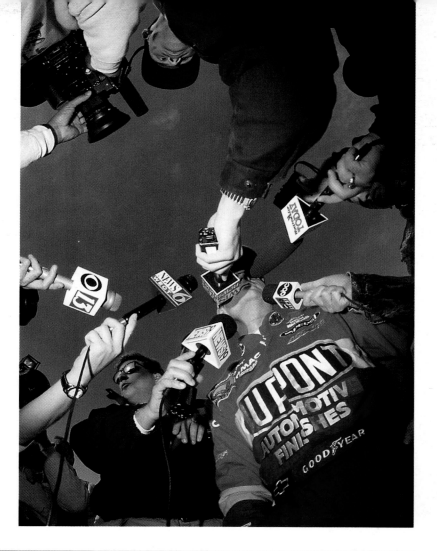

In the final quarter of the race, Jeff began to make the Rock's upper groove work for his Chevy. "I finally started to feel the high groove," he said. "There's a certain feeling you get." And on lap 350, in turns three and four, Jarrett "kinda slid up and tried to block me," Jeff said. "I turned underneath him." Jeff took the lead (above) on lap 351. It was the first time he had led the race. He was in front the rest of the way.

For the first time since David Pearson did it in 1976, a driver had won the first two races of the season. As he came out of his car, Jeff was on the phone again with Rick Hendrick. Then he raised the phone, and his owner's voice, high in the air. Later, Jeff lifted the Rock trophy skyward as Brooke, his wife, gave him a kiss, and the team gathered for the traditional group photograph.

After his team pushed his car through NASCAR inspection at Richmond International Raceway, Jeff finished fourth, behind three Fords, in the Pontiac Excitement 400.

At Atlanta Motor Speedway, Jeff posed (opposite) with the King, Richard Petty, the greatest winner in NASCAR history. But Jeff's fortunes turned sour in the Primestar 500. On lap 59, he slowed, drove onto pit road, and went behind pit wall (above). A string of oil trailed his car. "It was like a huge rumbling, a huge explosion under the hood," Jeff said. "I could tell it was coming out of the bottom. It felt like it was a (connecting) rod. It blew up and it blew up big." He finished 42nd—his worst finish of the year. And he dropped from first to fourth in points.

At Darlington Raceway, crew chief Ray Evernham and NASCAR official Brian DeHart select the all-important pit road position. Before the TranSouth 400, Jeff had time to perfect his free-throw form and have an amiable chat with Dale Jarrett, whose transporter was parked next to Jeff's. Jarrett won the race. Jeff finished third—behind two Fords.

In the inaugural Interstate Batteries 400 at Texas Motor Speedway, Jeff had led 69 laps and was running second when Ernie Irvan crashed at the start-finish line on lap 163. Jeff had nowhere to go. He hit Irvan's car, spun to a stop on pit road, then climbed out and inspected the damage. Back in the garage, Jeff and Ray discussed the extent of damage while the crew made repairs. Then he returned to the race. He finished 30th and dropped to fifth in NASCAR Winston Cup points—his lowest ranking of the year.

"To me, every race I do not win is a disappointment.

There seems to be more disappointments than victories in this sport. I know I've had my share."

THE FOOD CITY 500
BRISTOL MOTOR SPEEDWAY

Besides Wallace, Jeff's competition at the front included Dale Jarrett. During a round of pit stops, Jeff beat Jarrett out of the pits, then raced him under lengthening shadows. Ironically, while Jarrett was in the top five most of the race, he did not lead a lap.

At the bull ring known as Bristol Motor Speedway, Jeff passed Rusty Wallace on the last turn of the last lap for one of his greatest victories. "It was definitely the most exciting finish I've ever had in my career," he said. Gordon led 125 of the 500 laps and was in front before this restart around lap 200.

Wallace was in front from laps 415 through 499. He was in command—until the last lap. Here is how Jeff described it: "Not only was I trying to get by Rusty, but I was having to worry about Terry. I was almost protecting second more than trying to win it. The white flag came out and we came up on some cars and all of a sudden I got a great run off turn two and came right up on him. I wasn't touching him as we went into three but he got a little loose and we did touch. I dove under and we rubbed off of four to the checkered flag.

"Sometimes pure desire overcomes anything out there and you do everything it takes to get to Victory Lane."

It was Jeff's third straight victory in the Food City 500.

"Brooke helps me keep everything in perspective. She's not only my wife, she's my best friend."

THE GOODY'S 500

MARTINSVILLE SPEEDWAY

Bumping and shoving are part of the show at Martinsville Speedway, where Jeff and Ray discussed strategy before qualifications. Jeff qualified fourth and took the lead for the first time on lap 21. He led the next 307 laps.

"Ray and I are in sync.
He thinks the way I do about race cars;
how I want them to feel and drive. It's
like we are always on the same page."

Jeff led 432 of the 500 laps. "It wasn't smooth sailing," he said afterwards. "I got a few love taps myself today." The biggest one came from Jimmy Spencer on lap 328. Jeff was lapping Spencer in turns three and four when they collided. Both went spinning. Bobby Hamilton squeezed by and took the lead. On the radio, Jeff was cool. "It's getting wild," he said.

Less than 50 laps after the spin, Jeff pulled inside of Hamilton to challenge for the lead. They battled side-by-side for a lap and a half until Gordon slipped ahead for good in the first turn of lap 376.

"The whole day could have been over right when I spun. What saved it was that no one hit me, and I didn't damage the car. We were pretty lucky."

When he crossed the finish line, Jeff had pulled away to beat Hamilton by 1.047 seconds. A crowd of more than 70,000 watched as he turned into Victory Lane. As Unocal's Bill Brodrick and Motor Racing Network's Jim Phillips look on, Jeff raised his arms in a victory salute. Later, he shares a hug with Papa Joe Hendrick, Rick Hendrick's father.

In the remarkable, caution-free Winston 500 at Talladega Superspeedway, Jeff led 13 laps before finishing fifth, in part because of the quick pit stops of the Rainbow Warriors (right).

THE WINSTON
CHARLOTTE MOTOR SPEEDWAY

Above: For The Winston, Jeff unveiled a special Jurassic Park car
and a uniform to match to promote "Jurassic Park: The Ride." In
the afternoon, after he and Ray met by the car *(opposite)*, it was
clear from practice that he had a strong car. But Jeff was too fast
on his approach to the pits for the required stop during qualifying.
He took the green flag in the 19th and last starting position.

The bad starting spot simply gave Jeff an opportunity to display the prehistoric power of his car. He went from 19th to third in the first 30-lap segment. The field was inverted for the second 30 laps, so he restarted 17th. He led the way to the front, cutting a path for the fast cars as he passed competitors high and low.

For the final 10-lap sprint, Jeff started fourth on the outside of the second row. He dove under Bobby Labonte in turn three of the first lap to take second place. On the next lap, he made the same move in the same place to polish off Terry Labonte, and the race as well. His victory touched off a raucous celebration in Victory Lane.

"I don't go out thinking that we are going to win every race.

But if you go into a race thinking that you can't win, then you're already one step behind."

THE COCA-COLA 600
CHARLOTTE MOTOR SPEEDWAY

Center: Just before the race, as before every race, Jeff and Brooke pause for a moment of prayer. At left is the Rev. Max Helton of Motor Racing Outreach.

Bottom: If it's Charlotte, the celebrities will come, including Craig T. Nelson, the star of the television show "Coach." Nelson is a racer and an avid fan.

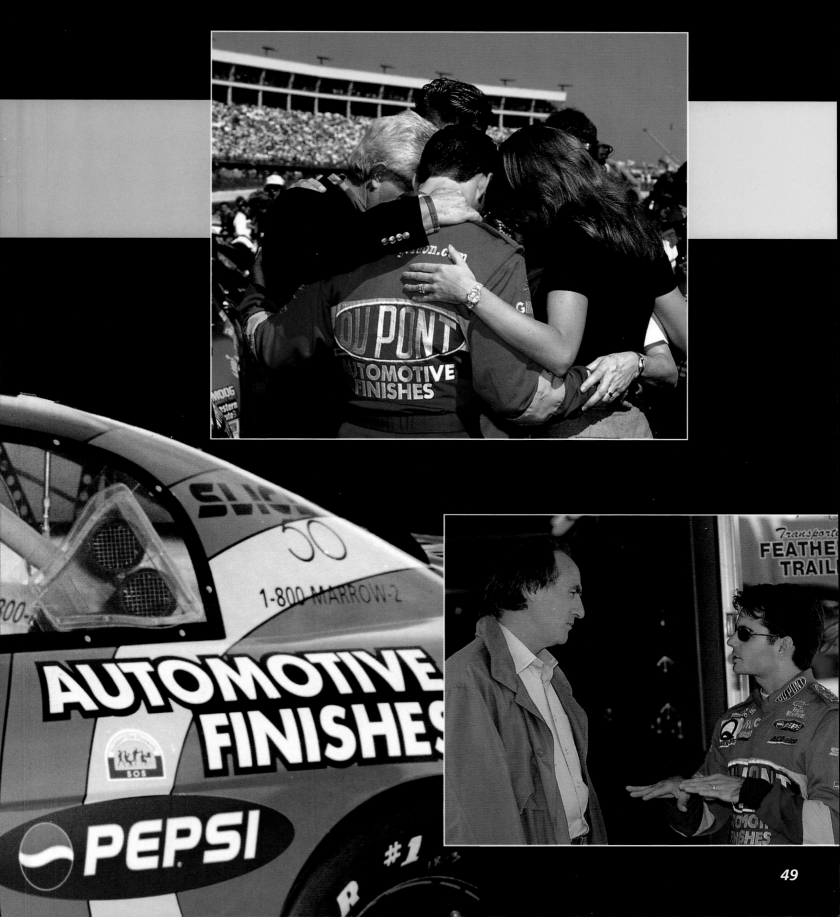

The pole allowed Jeff to lead 17 of the first 27 laps. But trouble soon struck, this time in the pits. His car fell off the jack on his first pit stop, damaging the body work behind the left front wheel well. He had to stop again for repairs and dropped to 38th.

With the help of four cautions and fast pit stops by his steady crew, Gordon made his way back through the field and was running third when rain interrupted the race on lap 195. In this spectacular night view, front tire changer Mike Trower clears out of the way as the crew sends Jeff back to the track after a two-tire pit stop.

Rain delayed the race and cooled the track. The chassis setup on Jeff's car, which had made the Chevy loose and hard to handle in the daylight hours, was perfect for night racing. A few minutes before 1 a.m. on May 26, with 17 laps remaining, Gordon made the race-winning pass on Rusty Wallace in the tri-oval.

"I've had a lot of success, but I feel like I'm still down-to-earth. I try to keep things in perspective. I feel I'm still the same person I was before my success; I'm just more mature and experienced now, not only in driving a car, but also off the track."

Reality returned to Jeff's racing world in the Miller 500 at Dover
Downs International Speedway. He was running second and in good
position to win when leader Dale Jarrett slowed for a spin. Jeff ran
into the back of him and punched a hole in his radiator. He lost 10
laps while his crew repaired the damage. He finished 26th.

THE POCONO 500
POCONO INTERNATIONAL RACEWAY

Jeff's victory in the Pocono 500 was his eighth win in 16 starts, counting The Winston and the Busch Clash. His phenomenal success earned him many new fans—and plenty of boos from the fans of other drivers. But when he was signing autographs, as he did behind the pits at Pocono *(below)*, not one fan had a harsh word to say.

Opposite: As he hoisted his new trophy in Victory Lane, Brooke was at his side, as well as Miss Winston, Renee Perks. The victory moved Jeff back into the NASCAR Winston Cup points lead for the first time since the race in Richmond in early March.

"My fans are awesome. *When you see how long they'll wait in a line for an autograph or picture, you realize how much it means to them. I don't think of myself as a celebrity or superstar, so to see people look up to me that way I find overwhelming."*

Jeff wiped out his primary car in a crash during practice the day before the Miller 400 at Michigan Speedway. He started from the rear of the field. But on the wide two-mile track, sometimes racing four wide, he moved to the front and eventually finished fifth.

CALIFORNIA 500
CALIFORNIA SPEEDWAY

On a bright Friday morning in Southern California, Jeff's crew pushes his car to the garage as the team prepares for the inaugural race at the new track.

In the garage paddock, Jeff chatted with NASCAR President Bill France between practice sessions. He also spent time comparing notes with teammate and friend Ricky Craven.

CALIFORNIA SPE

Jeff qualified third and took the lead for the first time on lap 24. He led 71 of the first 100 laps before giving way to Dale Jarrett. Later, teammate Terry Labonte would lead 41 laps.

www.NASCAR.NASCAR.COM

Jeff's crew serviced his car with the usual skill. And on the speedway, he battled at one point with Ernie Irvan. But in the end, it became a gas mileage battle. Jeff and his team found a new way to win. Even though his DuPont Chevy was supposed to run out of gas on the last lap, the engine kept singing its fight song right under the checkered flag. Jeff said the final circuit "was probably the slowest lap I made all day long. I've never really been a part of a fuel mileage contest and made it go all the way. I learned a lot about how to save and conserve fuel and win a race in a different fashion."

After battling with Dale Earnhardt in the Pepsi 400 at Daytona International Speedway, Jeff smacked the wall coming off turn two late in the race and limped home in 21st place. At Pocono later that month, Jeff enjoyed a moment with the seven-time champion before driver introductions.

Although a comment from Ray Evernham led to a moment of levity at New Hampshire International Speedway, Jeff had one of his poorest races of the year in the Jiffy Lube 300. He qualified 29th and finished 23rd, two laps down. Terry Labonte once again took the lead in the NASCAR Winston Cup championship.

Jeff was back on track at Pocono for the Pennsylvania 500, where he rubbed quarter panels with Dale Jarrett coming out of the third turn. The Ford driver eventually pulled ahead and won by almost three seconds, but Jeff finished second and retook the lead in points.

At the Indianapolis Motor Speedway, Jeff struggled in qualifying and started the Brickyard 400 from the 24th starting spot. But he ran a steady race, his crew gave him reliable, fast work in the pits, and he finished fourth, the best of the lot among the Chevy drivers.

"It was a dream of mine to go race at the Indianapolis 500, and when I went to NASCAR I thought my chances were gone. When they announced the inaugural Brickyard 400 for 1994, I was ecstatic. I don't think I ever wanted something so badly than to win that inaugural. Winning it was one of the greatest feelings I ever had in racing. I'll never forget it."

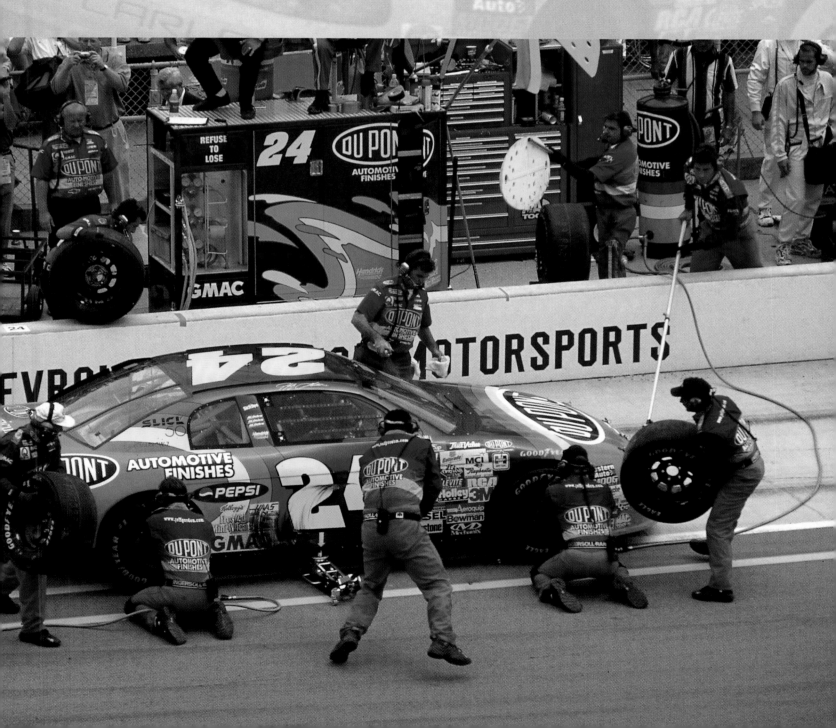

BUD AT THE GLEN
WATKINS GLEN INTERNATIONAL

"Brooke and I try to do things normal people would do. We like to go out to dinner, see movies, relax at home watching TV. Just being together and having personal time away from the race track is very important to us. We like to share that time together and not think about racing."

Upstate New York can be delightful in August, particularly at Watkins Glen International. Before going to battle on the track, Jeff took a stroll with Brooke through the garage paddock.

Jeff started 11th and battled his way through the field, racing with Dale Earnhardt and Sterling Marlin, among others. He took the lead for the first time on lap 53 of the 90-lap race.

Jeff led the final 27 laps to win the first road course victory of his NASCAR Winston Cup career. But it was a tough fight all the way, sometimes with Dale Earnhardt, sometimes with others.

In the ITW Devilbiss 400 at Michigan Speedway, gas man Mike Belden refuels the car during one of the pit stops Jeff made on his way to finishing second behind winner Mark Martin. It was Jeff's third (and last) runner-up finish of the season.

Jeff was dominating the Goody's 500 at Bristol Motor Speedway when trouble struck halfway through the race. On a restart on lap 245, Geoff Bodine blocked the low groove in turns one and two in his lapped car. Jeff pushed high in the turn and briefly slowed. When he gassed it, he and Jeremy Mayfield arrived at the same spot, exiting turn two at the same time, and the two cars collided like two outfielders chasing the same fly ball. Jeff limped to the pits with Mayfield trailing him. His crew tried to repair the car, but he eventually dropped out, finishing 35th. At the end of the night, he was trailing Mark Martin in the NASCAR Winston Cup points championship by 13 points.

THE SOUTHERN 500
DARLINGTON RACEWAY

The Mountain Dew Southern 500 starts the final 10 races of the season—the stretch run for the NASCAR Winston Cup championship. It was now a horse race, and Jeff wasn't even leading anymore. The pressure at Darlington was particularly intense, for if Jeff could win the Southern 500 after his victories in the Daytona 500 and the Coca-Cola 600, he would join Bill Elliott as the only other driver to win the Winston Million. His crew put special "Million Dollar Date" decals on his car and wore special T-shirts.

"It takes key people to make things work, and to me, the Rainbow Warriors are the most important part of all of this. They are an awesome team and the ones who really make it happen. They believe in each other and do whatever it takes to win. That's quite a commitment, so I feel it's important for me to give back that same commitment."

DARLING

The team brought Jeff's "Million Dollar Date" car to Darlington. He ran well in practice and qualified seventh.

In the race, Jeff took the lead for the first time on lap 72. Dale Jarrett was in the thick of things, as usual, and Geoff Bodine, while not among the leaders, was still not to be taken lightly, as he had demonstrated at Bristol. And on lap 167, Jeff made it safely past the spinning car of Ward Burton in turn two.

Jeff's most persistent competitor during the race was Ford driver Bill Elliott, who led 181 laps—more than anyone. But Elliott faded when clouds moved in and the track tightened. Jeff's Chevy improved. So did Jeff Burton's Ford. Jeff took the lead on lap 296. His pit stops were consistent and fast, including the final stop on lap 335. But in Burton's pit, a lug nut fell off a wheel during a tire change. He dropped from third to seventh. Burton sliced back through the field, but he did not challenge Jeff for the lead until the last two laps of the race.

In the final laps, the handling on Jeff's Chevy became almost impossibly tight. "I was just trying to stay out of the wall," he said. "I almost had to use the wall to turn." Burton made his charge as the cars came off turn four to take the white flag. "I saw him coming, so I moved left to slow down his momentum," he said. The cars came together as they crossed the line. In the process, Burton's tires became covered with loose sand, rock, and rubber. "We ran door to door, banging all the way down the front stretch," Jeff said. "And by the time we got to [turn] one, he had to let up. His tires were like ice." Jeff crossed the finish line two car lengths ahead of Burton.

After Jeff was escorted to Victory Lane by a pace car and an armored truck, he emerged from his car to lead the biggest celebration since Daytona. It was not so much the million-dollar bonus as the fact that it had been won only once before, by Bill Elliott in 1985. And it was the way Jeff won it, holding off a frantic last-lap challenge while trying to drive an ill-handling car.

"It's one thing to win a race like this if you've got a great car and you dominate the day," Jeff said. "But to finish first and to have a great battle while driving a car that wasn't the best handling car on the track that day—that was really something else."

Overshadowed by all this was the fact that it was Jeff's third straight victory in the Southern 500—an unprecedented feat in NASCAR's oldest superspeedway race.

The victory at Darlington propelled Jeff back on top in the battle for the NASCAR Winston Cup championship. And at Richmond International Raceway, where a pensive Jeff paused between practice sessions, a third-place finish in the Exide Batteries Select 400 gave him a 97-point lead over Mark Martin.

CMT 300
NEW HAMPSHIRE INTERNATIONAL SPEEDWAY

Previous page: Jeff's teammate Ricky Craven had the measure of the field and led most of the first half of the race along with Pontiac driver Bobby Hamilton. Jeff stayed near the front with the help of good pit stops on a crowded pit road. He took the lead for the first time on lap 149 of the 300-lap race. And he took the lead for good on lap 228.

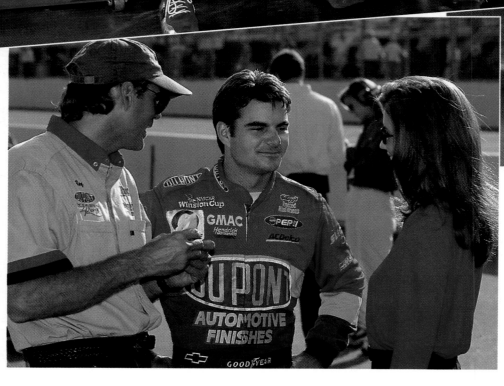

Left: The pressure-packed points battle did not stop Jeff and Mark Martin from having a friendly chat at New Hampshire. And on pit road before the race, he was relaxed while standing with Brooke and Ray Evernham.

Jeff, shown here passing Kenny Wallace, was able to keep the field behind him in the final third of the race. But during the last pit stop, crew chief Ray Evernham made a bold decision to maintain the lead by sending Jeff back out on old tires. Despite the disadvantage, Jeff managed to hold off Ernie Irvan. "I know my little buddy has a ton of talent," Ray said. "We lean on that when we need to."

For the 10th time, Jeff and his team went to Victory Lane. For the 10th time, they posed for the seemingly endless array of publicity photos. Jeff and Brooke acknowledged that achievement with their hands while celebrating in Victory Lane. What they did not know was that the 10th time was the last time for 1997. They were done winning races, but the biggest challenge—the toughest hurdle—remained.

The next stop was Dover Downs International Raceway. Jeff, shown here under the care of the Rainbow Warriors in the pits, did what he had to do in the MBNA 400—he survived. He finished seventh, two laps down. Mark Martin won on gas mileage and trailed Jeff by 105 points.

"I always take one race at a time.

I try not to look too far ahead. If you do that you tend to lose sight of what is happening now. Which, in racing, can be very dangerous."

Above: In the Hanes 500 at Martinsville Speedway, Jeff led Jeff Burton, Dale Earnhardt, and Mark Martin out of the pits after a round of stops. Jeff led 21 laps, but faded to fourth. Burton won, Earnhardt finished second. Martin was 11th. Jeff's lead over Martin in the NASCAR Winston Cup championship stretched to 135 points.

Left: In the UAW-GM 500 at Charlotte Motor Speedway, the three points leaders—Jeff, Mark Martin and Dale Jarrett—put on a show as they battled each other for position. Jeff never led a lap in this race, but he finished fifth, one spot behind Martin. Jarrett won the race and moved to within 197 points of the lead. Jeff's lead over Martin slipped to 125 points.

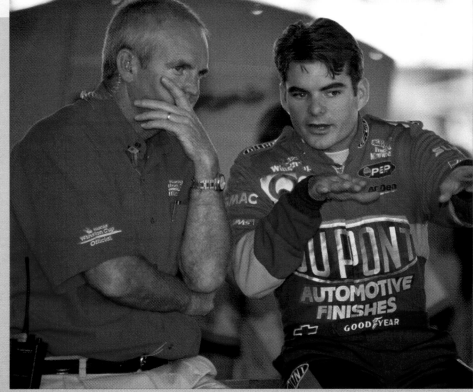

At Talladega Superspeedway for the DieHard 500, Jeff and Dale Earnhardt *(above)* shared a laugh. And Jeff spent some time in serious conversation with NASCAR Winston Cup Director Gary Nelson *(right)*. In the race, Jeff led three early laps and was holding steady near the front of a double-wide pack of cars when disaster struck. A tire went down on his Chevy, sending him into John Andretti's car, then into the wall. Almost the entire field had nowhere to go. When the crash was over, 23 cars were involved, including both Mark Martin and Dale Jarrett, as well as Earnhardt. Jeff returned to the track in his crippled car, but only completed 153 of the 188 laps and finished 35th. There was little change in the points. Martin was now 110 behind. Jarrett trailed by 155.

"This is a job. You can't worry too much about the dangers. And when you've done it as much as I have, you start to get used to the speeds. You're just trying to focus on getting out there and going fast. You don't think about if there is going to be a wreck. You basically have to get in there and do what you do every weekend."

In the pits at North Carolina Speedway for the
AC Delco 400, Brooke stayed tuned into Jeff's
radio channel with earphones. In the race itself,
Jeff led Dale Jarrett and teammate Terry
Labonte. Jarrett finished second. Jeff was fourth.
Mark Martin finished sixth.

Jeff was motoring along in his usual zone in the Dura-Lube 500 at Phoenix International Raceway *(opposite)*, solidly positioned in fifth place, when misfortune struck again. A right front tire began vibrating. It blew out with less than 50 laps to go. "There were over 2,000 tires here today and we got the only one that had a problem," Ray Evernham said afterwards.

Although two laps down in 30th after his emergency stop, Jeff mounted an incredible comeback and finished 17th, saving 39 crucial points in the NASCAR Winston Cup championship battle. Dale Jarrett, who won the race, moved into second, 77 points behind. Martin finished sixth and was 87 points back. Now the challenge was clear. Jeff had to finish 18th or better at Atlanta. But after Talladega and Phoenix, it seemed that anything could happen. "I don't know what to expect these days," Jeff said.

THE NAPA 500
ATLANTA MOTOR SPEEDWAY

The tension of the NAPA 500 weekend at Atlanta Motor Speedway is reflected in the image of Ray Evernham *(right)* during the race. After qualifications were rained out Friday, Jeff was headed down pit road first thing Saturday morning when he made a "bonehead move," as he described it. He was sawing the steering wheel back and forth, trying to warm his tires on a cold, gray morning, when the tires lost their grip altogether and the car took off on him. Jeff spun around and slammed into Bobby Hamilton's car. Both drivers had to use backup cars for qualifying, where Jeff had more trouble. He started the race 37th.

"Sometimes I feel bad for Ray because *his job as crew chief is so time consuming it takes him away from his family. When we get the chance, we like to sit down and just talk about things. He's really a good person."*

Jeff and Ray did their best to try to dig themselves out of their hole, but the weekend at times seemed scripted from a horror movie. During the race itself, Jeff found himself mired among the backmarkers. His car was not handling well. In the pits, Ray was a bundle of nerves. In the car, Jeff was nervous, but ready to face the challenge.

ATLANTA

The ordeal lasted three hours and eight minutes. But moments after race winner Bobby Labonte took the checkered flag, Jeff flashed across the line as well. He was in 17th place and he was only 14 points ahead of Dale Jarrett. But after months of points counting, the final tally really didn't matter. Jeff was the 1997 NASCAR Winston Cup champion. And that was all that counted.

"Defending the NASCAR Winston Cup champion-ship during NASCAR's 50th anniversary is very exciting. The sport has really moved up to a another level and I'm proud to be part of it. I look forward to what it's going to be like at the 100th anniversary. I hope I'm still around to celebrate."

Opposite: Jeff started his victory celebration with his own impromptu celebration at the finish line on top of his car. In Victory Lane, Jeff and Brooke shared a kiss.

NASCAR
Winston Cup
Series

#24
HENDRICK MOTORSPORTS

1997
NASCAR WINSTON CUP CHAMPION
JEFF GORDON

It was a season to be savored, despite the untidy ending. And as Jeff faced the media once again, he could not help repeating how thankful, and how blessed, he was. *Opposite:* A triumphant Jeff at the victory celebration in New York City.